I AM AN ACTIVIST!

COLORING BOOK

CASEY CHAPMAN ROSS

ISBN: 978-1-7340503-0-1 Paperback
ISBN: 978-1-7340503-1-8 Ebook

c c r
press

THANK YOU!

EXTRA SPECIAL THANKS TO LEO IN AUSTIN, TX.
YOUR COURAGE ON MARCH 27TH, 2019
INSPIRED ME TO FIND WAYS TO HELP OTHER
YOUNG PEOPLE FIND THEIR VOICE.

ALSO VERY GRATEFUL TO:

MUNA, SAMIR, MEESHA & JIBREEL

LARA DREW AND HAYDEN AKTARY

CHRIS, JEN, COOPER, JUNA AND AIDEN CHAPMAN

RICH AND NATE DEPALMA

DIANA MARIE EARL

JESSICA MANGRUM AND JOHN & VIVIENNE FORD

TIFFANY HARELIK

HENRY HASERT

SHELLIE HAYES-MCMAHON

TERRY HELLER

MARGARET CHEN AND XANDER, KASSIE & MAX KERCHER

SUSANNE & ZOE KERNS

RACHEL AND LILY LACLAIRE

CONNOLLY COYLE AND JON, BREDA & HENRY LEES

VANESSA REISER

LIAM, LOGAN AND ZOEY ROSS

LOUIE & LINDEN RIESCH AND KENNON WOOTEN

DEEDS NOT WORDS

VOTING IS A RIGHT
THAT SHOULD BE PRACTICED
AT EVERY OPPORTUNITY.
YOUR VOTE AND
YOUR VOICE MATTER.

DO YOUR PART TO
STAY INFORMED
ABOUT WHAT IS HAPPENING
IN YOUR COMMUNITY.

LET OTHERS KNOW
HOW YOU FEEL.
DON'T BE AFRAID
TO SPEAK YOUR MIND!

EVEN WHEN YOU MAY BE
SHY OR SCARED,
BE TRUE TO YOURSELF.

YOUR VISION IS
ONE OF A KIND!
HOW CAN YOUR TALENT
HELP OTHERS?

GET OUT THE VOTE! HELP REMIND AND EDUCATE OTHERS WHEN AND WHERE TO VOTE.

TREAT OTHERS
THE WAY YOU WISH
TO BE TREATED.

BE SOMEONE'S CHAMPION.

WHEN A FRIEND IS
BEING BRAVE,
STAND BY THEIR SIDE.

WHEN HELP IS NEEDED, JUMP IN!

KEEP YOUR HEAD HIGH!
YOU CAN'T WIN THEM ALL
BUT THAT DOESN'T MEAN YOU
SHOULD STOP TRYING.

LOVE
ALWAYS
OVERCOMES
HATE.

YOU ARE NOT ALONE.
SHARE YOUR FEELINGS
WITH SOMEONE YOU LOVE.

IMAGINE HOW
SOMEONE ELSE
IS FEELING.

BEING A GOOD LISTENER
IS A BIG PART OF
BEING A GOOD FRIEND.

ASKING QUESTIONS
IS HOW WE
LEARN NEW THINGS.
THERE ARE NO
SILLY QUESTIONS!

WHEN YOU HAVE MORE THAN ENOUGH, SHARE WITH OTHERS LESS FORTUNATE.

DON'T FORGET TO
HAVE FUN
AND FIND JOY
IN THE THINGS
THAT YOU DO!

DRAW A PICTURE
OF YOURSELF!
YOU
ARE
AWESOME!

PROUD

ACTIVIST!

CASEY CHAPMAN ROSS
AUTHOR

CASEY CHAPMAN ROSS LIVES IN AUSTIN, TEXAS WITH HER HUSBAND AND THREE KIDS. AS HER OWN CHILDREN GROW, SO DOES CASEY'S PASSION FOR EDUCATING A YOUNG AUDIENCE ON BECOMING MORE COMMUNITY-MINDED, CIVICALLY ENGAGED HUMANS. CASEY BELIEVES THE MORE WE INVOLVE OUR KIDS IN OUR OWN PASSIONS AND ACTIVISM, THE MORE A YOUNG GENERATION WILL CARE TO GET INVOLVED. CASEY IS ALSO A FREELANCE PHOTOGRAPHER FOCUSING ON PROGRESSIVE CAMPAIGNS, CANDIDATES, AND GROUPS THROUGHOUT THE COUNTRY TO EMBOLDEN THEIR VOICE THROUGH POWERFUL IMAGERY.

ZOE KERNS

ZOE KERNS IS A FRESHMAN AT THE MCCALLUM FINE ARTS ACADEMY IN AUSTIN, TEXAS. SHE MOVED TO AUSTIN FROM SEATTLE WITH HER PARENTS AND LITTLE BROTHER NINE YEARS AGO AND IS STILL HAPPIEST WHEN THE FORECAST CALLS FOR CLOUDS AND RAIN. IN 2018, ZOE PARTNERED WITH A FRENCH STUDENT TO ILLUSTRATE HIS STORY WHICH WAS PERFORMED FOR A LIVE AUDIENCE AT LE GRAND SPECTACLE WITH THE FRENCH FEDERATION OF DYSLEXIA. HER PASSION FOR ANIMALS HAS LED HER TO BE A SUPPORTER OF AUSTIN PETS ALIVE WHERE SHE ENJOYS FOSTERING, (AND ADOPTING) RESCUE DOGS, LIKE HER DOGS BEAR AND DAISY. WHETHER MARCHING, OR SIMPLY WEARING HER VALUES ON A T-SHIRT, SHE IS PROUD TO SPEAK UP ON BEHALF OF MARGINALIZED VOICES IN HER COMMUNITY.

GLOSSARY OF TERMS

NOTE TO PARENTS AND TEACHERS: SOME TERMS FOUND IN THIS COLORING BOOK MAY BE NEW CONCEPTS FOR YOUR CHILD OR STUDENT. DEFINITIONS AND WORD USAGE EXAMPLES ARE PROVIDED HERE TO HELP YOUNG CITIZENS LEARN MORE ABOUT SOME OF THE TERMS USED BY THOSE WHO ARE ACTIVE PARTICIPANTS IN THE DEMOCRATIC PROCESS.

ACTIVIST: ONE WHO PURSUES A POLITICAL OR SOCIAL CHANGE // "I AM AN ACTIVIST WITH MY SCOUT TROOP—WE ARE GETTING ALL OF THE SCOUTS FROM OUR AREA TO TALK TO THE CITY COUNCIL ABOUT THE NEED FOR BETTER ANIMAL SHELTERS."

ADVOCATE: ONE WHO SPEAKS OR ACTS ON BEHALF OF SOMEONE ELSE // "I TALKED TO THE PRINCIPAL AT SCHOOL ABOUT MAKING THE PLAYGROUND SURFACE SMOOTHER AND MORE WHEELCHAIR-FRIENDLY. I AM AN ADVOCATE FOR MY HANDICAPPED CLASSMATE BEING ABLE TO GO OUTSIDE WITH THE REST OF THE CLASS FOR RECESS."

EMPATHY: UNDERSTANDING AND SHARING THE FEELINGS OF ANOTHER // "I CAN EMPATHIZE WITH MY CLASSMATE FROM GUATEMALA TRYING TO FIGURE OUT ENGLISH WORDS DURING READING BECAUSE SOMETIMES I HAVE TROUBLE FIGURING OUT HOW TO WORK PROBLEMS IN MATH."

GOTV: GET OUT THE VOTE—ORGANIZED EFFORTS TO ENCOURAGE PEOPLE TO VOTE // "I GET TO PUT THE GOTV DOOR HANGARS ON EVERY HOUSE WHEN I GO WITH MY MOM AND DAD TO REMIND PEOPLE TO VOTE."

OPTIMISM: CONFIDENCE AND HOPEFULNESS ABOUT FUTURE OUTCOMES // "EVEN WHEN TIMES ARE DIFFICULT, I AM OPTIMISTIC THAT WE CAN WORK TOGETHER AND MAKE THINGS BETTER."

RIGHT TO VOTE: THE RIGHT TO CAST A BALLOT IN AN ELECTION // "BEFORE 1918, ONLY MEN WERE ALLOWED TO VOTE IN THE UNITED STATES. BUT WITH PASSAGE OF THE 19TH AMENDMENT TO THE CONSTITUTION, WOMEN FINALLY GAINED THE RIGHT TO VOTE."

"SHOW UP": BEING PRESENT FOR AN ACTIVITY OR GATHERING // "WHEN VOLUNTEERS ARE NEEDED ON A CAMPAIGN, I SHOW UP—I BELIEVE IN DOING MY PART IN A DEMOCRACY."

SOLIDARITY: PEOPLE STANDING TOGETHER FOR THE SAME IDEAS, FEELINGS OR ACTIONS // "I SHOWED SOLIDARITY WITH MY FRIEND WHEN I STOOD BY HIM IN SUPPORT AS HE SPOKE TO THE CLASS ABOUT BEING CAREFUL AROUND GUNS."

"SPEAK UP": EXPRESS ONE'S FEELINGS OR OPINIONS FRANKLY AND PUBLICLY // "WHEN I SEE A FRIEND IS BEING BULLIED ON THE PLAYGROUND, I DON'T THINK IT'S RIGHT, AND I SPEAK UP FOR HIM BY TELLING A GROWN UP."

VOLUNTEERISM: WORKING FOR AN ORGANIZATION OR CAUSE WITHOUT BEING PAID // "I AM A VOLUNTEER AT THE LIBRARY EACH WEEK TO HELP OUT BY READING STORIES TO YOUNGER CHILDREN."

CPSIA information can be obtained
at www.ICGtesting.com
Printed in the USA
LVHW101415110221
679066LV00036B/341

9 781734 050301